Hanna-Barbera's
**THE GREATEST ADVENTURE**
STORIES FROM THE BIBLE

# JOSHUA
## AND
## THE BATTLE
## OF JERICHO

text by
**Christine L. Benagh**

*Based on a script by Harvey Bullock*

ABINGDON PRESS
*Nashville*

Two young friends, Derek and Margo, are taking part in a very important dig in the Middle East. It is the opportunity of a lifetime for them to accompany her father, an archaeologist, on this expedition.

Most days their young nomad friend Moki, who is very curious about these things, joins them to ask a hundred questions and to keep things generally lively.

One especially hot and tiring day, the three friends are digging in their assigned spot, when the sand suddenly begins to give way. "Quick sand," shouts Moki as the three

JOSHUA AND THE BATTLE OF JERICHO

ISBN 0-687-15743-9

MANUFACTURED BY THE PARTHENON PRESS AT NASHVILLE, TENNESSEE, UNITED STATES OF AMERICA

spiral down, down, down in a funnel of
sand.

Then just as unexpectedly the air is clear,
and they are in an enormous room. What a
spectacle! It is filled with treasure of every
sort—vases, jars, statues, jewelry and
ornaments, pillars, furniture of gold and
ivory.

"How magnificent," whispers Derek in
awe.

"Wow," murmurs Moki.

Margo has moved ahead of the others
toward a huge bronze door. The latch
fastening the two massive panels is a
golden scarab beetle. She puts her hand on
the scarab, translating its message: *All who
enter here go back in time.* Suddenly, the
great doors swing open into what appears
to be a cavern of light.

"Come on," she calls, and without
hesitation the others follow.

They step over the threshold and —

Moki, Margo, and Derek found
themselves standing in a quiet
green countryside with soft rolling hills and
here and there a stand of trees.

"Where do you suppose we are?" Margo
wondered aloud.

Derek pointed ahead, "Perhaps if we
follow this track, it will lead us somewhere
to find out."

They set out at a slow but steady pace,
looking carefully on all sides for clues.
"Hold it!" Derek stopped. "I hear horses."

"Duck," said Moki, and they took cover
behind a clump of bushes.

Two powerful horses galloped by at top
speed drawing a chariot. The driver did not
spare them. He shouted and swore as he
whipped them into a lather. The pointed
helmet on his head perfectly matched his
fierce expression. Close behind came other
chariots.

When the last one had rumbled by, Moki
raised his head cautiously. "Who were
those guys?"

"From the looks of their clothing, I think
they may belong to some tribe in the land
of Palestine. They could well be Hittites,"
suggested Derek.

"Or some other tribe of the same
period," put in Margo, "Hivites,
Girgashites, Amorites, Jebusites, or perhaps
Canaanites."

Moki stared at his friends. "What about
socialites, suburbanites, parasites, or
satellites?"

"Zip the lip, Moki," Margo was laughing.
"At any rate I think we can say that we are
back one thousand years B.C."

Derek shushed them again. "More horses
are coming, and we want to steer clear of
everybody until we know where we are.
This is not much cover."

"For such empty country there sure is lots of traffic," piped Moki as he ran to the shelter of a large bramble some distance away. Margo and Derek plunged behind a bush closer to the path, and just in time, for two chariots drew up not twenty feet from their hiding place.

"There are definitely Israelite spies here, captain." The soldier in the lead chariot was speaking. "I saw them moving right about here."

The two men climbed out with swords drawn. They began thrusting and jabbing into the very bush where Margo and Derek crouched. A blade came ripping through the leaves only inches from Derek's face.

Watching from his own bush, Moki held his breath. He could do nothing to help his friends. They had not yet been seen, but those probing swords would find them soon. He bent low and began backing slowly out from under his bush, preparing to dash to a safer spot. He did not see the large thorn aimed right at the seat of his pants. It felt like a sword point, and he jumped and cried out in pain. "Ouch!" he yelped, jumping up. The two soldiers were on him in an instant.

"It's only a boy." The captain jerked him up roughly. "We know there are other spies here. Where are they?"

"Oh no," gasped Margo, "they have Moki."

"Poor guy. But he has saved us, at least for now." Derek grabbed her arm. "Come on. As long as we are free, we may be able to help him." They ran through a gap in the hills and took cover in a grove of trees on the other side of the ridge.

But the soldiers had seen them. They made for their chariots, dragging Moki with them. Other chariots had come to join the chase. "Israelite spies," shouted the captain. "You circle around on that side of the hill, and we will have them trapped against the river."

Margo and Derek thought the river might be their best chance to get away, but as they got nearer they saw that it was a torrent of surging flood water.

"I hear chariots, Derek. What will we do?"

"Grab that log," he shouted. "It's our only chance." As the log swept by they each caught a branch and ducked under the swirling current to surface on the other side. They went rushing downstream with only their noses above water.

The soldiers reined up at the river's edge. "I saw them go in, captain." They all surveyed the water carefully.

"There's no sign of them now," replied the officer. "They could not last in this current. They have drowned." Moki turned his head to hide the tears he could not keep back.

The captain nodded in his direction. "Take him into the city and put him to work on the walls."

Margo and Derek rode their strange boat for a long distance before they dared to raise their heads and look around. When they saw no sign of their pursuers, they steered the log to shore and crawled out onto the bank wet and exhausted.

"We made it, but poor Moki," sighed Margo.

Derek reassured her, "At least we managed to get away, that's what's important. We could not help him at all otherwise. Let's look for a safer place to hide."

They turned to climb the bank and gulped. Two strapping soldiers blocked the path, but these were soldiers of a different sort. They wore a soft sort of turban wrapped about the head with a cloth falling to the shoulders.

The officer standing behind spoke to the younger soldier. "They are probably spies. I will question them in my tent. Bring them along."

"Yes, Simeon." He took Margo and Derek firmly by the arm.

The officer questioned them for some time. "So you are not Canaanites. Please forgive us for taking you against your

will, but we Israelites must be very careful. We are in a strange country surrounded by people who are our enemies."

"Israelites!" Derek and Margo exclaimed together. "And those other soldiers are Canaanites?"

"Yes," replied Simeon. "They are from the great walled city just beyond the River Jordan. We are preparing to cross into the land of Canaan. We are to capture the city of Jericho."

"How are you going to cross that river?" asked Derek. "It's on a rampage."

"Ah, my young friend, it will take more than a river to stop us. The Lord our God has led us through the desert wilderness for forty years. He has brought us safely from Egypt to the borders of our Promised Land. Nothing can stop us now."

Margo interrupted. "When you take Jericho, will you rescue our friend Moki? He's a prisoner there."

"Of course. But look, Joshua is about to speak to the people. Let us go and listen. He is no doubt outlining the plans. If only Moses had lived to see this day. He is the one who brought us this far, and he himself named Joshua as our new leader."

They recognized Joshua easily. He had the look of a chieftain and was a head taller than the rest. The people gathered around as he mounted the stone steps leading to a platform.

"People of Israel, this is the day we have been waiting for. Today we will cross the River Jordan and enter the land that the Lord has promised us."

A cheer went up.

"You priests, men of the Levites, you will lead. You are to take up the Ark of the Covenant and march with it ahead of the people."

The priests moved toward the large box sitting to one side of the platform. A rich cloth covered it, and there were two golden poles run through rings of gold at the corners. That was all that could be seen of it. Four robed priests grasped the poles, lifted the ark, and moved with it toward the river. A long plaintive note sounded from the ram's horn trumpet. The other priests fell in line, and the procession solemnly moved forward.

"Look, Derek, there it is, the Ark of the Covenant. Do you know what is in it? The stone tablets with the Ten Commandments written on them."

"Wow!" He turned to Simeon, "Why are they doing this? Shouldn't there be soldiers guarding the ark? It could be captured."

"I only know that Joshua says he is doing all things as the Lord has commanded." His reply was interrupted by the ram's horn sounding a second time. The procession halted, and the four priests bearing the ark went on alone.

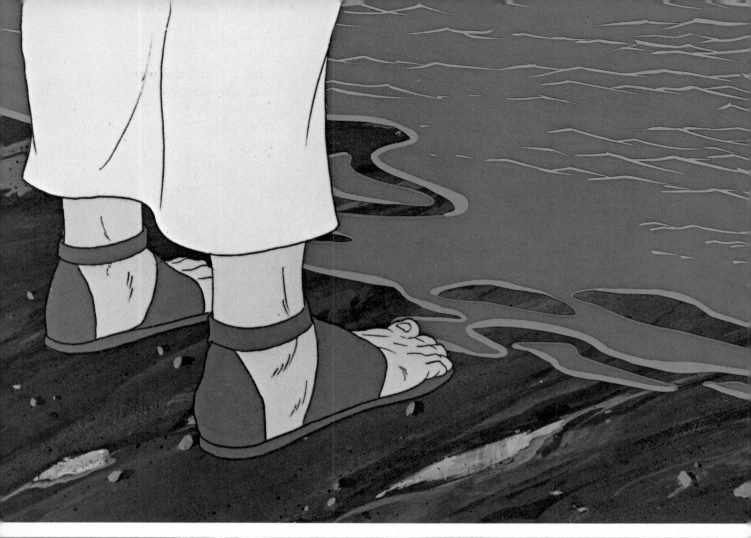

"They will never make it across with such a load," Derek whispered to Margo.

On the opposite side of the river, Canaanite lookouts were watching the procession with interest. "Look at them! The fools are going to try to cross the river. No one can cross that wild water now."

The captain laughed. "We will make quick work of any who have the bad luck not to drown."

"I do not understand, sir," a soldier spoke up. "Only four men are approaching the river, and they obviously are not soldiers. What are they carrying?"

As they neared the water's edge, Joshua appeared at the edge of the trees. He raised his arm to the priests. "Have no fear; move out steadily until you are in midstream. There you will stop. Trust in the Lord."

The men stepped into the swirling waters.

"I can't look." Derek turned to Margo.

"You must. Look what is happening! As they put their feet down, the water sinks and moves back. The water level is going down."

"It's just like the Red Sea parting for Moses," said Derek.

Simeon walked up to Joshua. "My men stand ready, sir."

The leader nodded. "Let them move forward when the river bed is completely dry."

The Canaanites also saw. "What is going on?" exclaimed one of the soldiers.

"They have been fooled by a trick current," the captain sneered. "Now watch as the waters rush in and drown them all."

"Look now, captain," another soldier exclaimed, "the river has dried up."

At this the Israelite soldiers gave a great cry and charged toward the dry river bed. The frightened Canaanites whirled and retreated at full speed into the walls of the city.

"Hang on, Moki!" Margo was jumping up and down. "Help is on the way."

Moki needed all the help he could get. He had been set to work carrying buckets of mortar and great bricks to strengthen and reinforce the walls of Jericho, walls that already seemed massive.

A soldier standing guard nearby commented to the overseer of the work detail, "Did you know that the people of Israel crossed the river three days ago? They are on the march toward our city."

"Have no fear, they can never get past our walls. They are the strongest in the land, and we are making them stronger."

Moki's heart plunged into his shoes.

The whole company of Israelites had crossed into the land of Canaan and made their camp close to the spot of their unforgettable crossing. The river was flowing normally again, and the people felt confident that God was guiding their way.

Simeon stood with Margo and Derek on a hillock and looked out over the pleasant scene. "This is truly a blessed land, so green and fertile. Our families will grow strong and healthy here."

"How far is it to Jericho?" asked Derek.

"About three miles. It is just beyond that row of hills."

"That's great," said Margo. "Your men can make that march in no time. When will you set out?"

"I cannot say." Simeon looked troubled. "I want to march now, and my soldiers are anxious. But Joshua has given different orders. The priests have rituals that must be performed, and then we are to keep the Passover."

"Passover! How long will that take?" asked Margo.

"Too long! We will lose our momentum and give the Canaanites time to make their walls so strong we can never get through. The Passover feast lasts seven days, valuable days we cannot afford to waste if we want to take the city."

Waiting was taking a toll on the Canaanites also. Behind their mighty walls, the king summoned the captain of his forces to the palace. "Where are the Israelites? Why do they not march? What are they up to?"

"They are not far from the city, Sire, but they are not marching. Our spy has just returned with the news that they are baking cakes for a festival."

"What strange people," the king shouted. "First they cross the raging River Jordan, and then they stop to eat *cakes*? I do not like this."

"Have no fear, O King, we are using every hour to strengthen our fortress." The captain bowed and made his exit.

Margo was worried. "If only there were some way to get word to Moki and let him know we will be coming soon."

Derek agreed. "He might do something desperate like trying to escape."

"The Canaanites would kill him if he failed," said Simeon. "Hmm . . . perhaps there is something you can do. Here comes the man who has been our spy inside the city. He may know how to get word to your friend. Jebron, here.

"These are some friends who need your help. Their young companion is a prisoner in Jericho. Is there some way they

could get a message inside to him?''

"There might be," responded the young man, "but it will be risky."

"We're almost used to that." Derek's laugh was nervous.

Jebron continued, "Perched on the wall of the city is the house of a woman named Rahab. She can be trusted. She sheltered me when I was there. She promised to be listening at her window every night in case we need her help."

Margo was excited. "That's great! We can wait until dark and make our way there."

"Good," said Jebron, "I will come with you to show the way and to point out her window."

Under the cover of darkness the little party set out. Margo and Derek had dark robes borrowed to conceal them on this mission. They picked their way carefully to an abandoned shepherd's hut. From here Jebron pointed out a dimly lit window atop the wall. "That is her window. Take care, I am going to leave you now. Two can hide more easily than three. Derek, you take my headpiece. Then Rahab will know you are one of us. Good luck." He disappeared.

Running noiselessly from one boulder to another, Derek and Margo reached their destination beneath the lighted window and stopped to look up.

"Oh no!" Margo pointed to a sentry standing silhouetted directly above them. He stopped to survey the scene and then moved away.

Derek picked up a rock and threw it toward the window, but his aim was off and the stone clattered noisily down the wall. The guard peered over the edge of the parapet. Derek threw another stone at a cluster of pigeons roosting on the ledge above them. They fluttered up with a whir, and the guard moved away satisfied.

"My baseball arm is out of practice." Taking careful aim, he let go again. This time the rock sailed through the window. In a moment a head appeared.

"Israel," whispered Margo.

Without a word the woman let down a knotted rope, and Derek climbed up while Margo steadied it below. He did not go inside, but spoke in low tones through the window.

"I understand," the woman said. "I am sure I can pick out your friend and give him the word that you are coming and to keep his hopes up."

"Thank you so much," said Derek. "We will be waiting in that hut by the road. You can give us a signal. Use that mirror on your table. Flash it once if you do not find him, flash two times if you do, and three times if he is all right."

Rahab nodded. "Can you tell me when the Israelites will march against the city?"

"I honestly don't know," said Derek and slipped quietly to the ground.

At the break of dawn next day Joshua came out of his tent and walked away from the encampment. He wanted to be alone to think and pray, for he was troubled. "Here we are safely in our Promised Land, and the army stands ready. But I do not know what we are to do now." He paced back and forth.

Suddenly in front of him and hovering just above the ground, there was a soldier with sword drawn. He looked like a man, but was much larger.

"Who are you? Where do you come from? Are you an enemy of Israel?"

"I am the Captain of the Angels of the Lord." His sword glistened in the morning light.

Joshua dropped to his knees and put his face to the ground. "Speak, Lord, for I am your servant. Command and I will obey."

Joshua hurried back to camp and summoned his officers and the priests and leaders of the people. "We have received our orders. This day we are to march."

The men nodded approval.

"Pay close attention," continued Joshua, "for these commands are from the Lord God. Seven priests are to take seven trumpets of ram's horn and go before the ark. A guard of armed men will march at the head, and the rest of the men of arms will march behind. This procession will circle the city one time. You are not to make a sound with your voice, not even a word. When you have completed the circuit, return to the camp in silence."

The group stood hushed and puzzled, and then they began to mumble.

"I cannot believe this." Simeon went striding away.

Rahab set about her task early that same morning. She strolled along the top of the walls twirling her bright scarf. She had spotted Moki, and she approached a sentry standing just above the work gang. She flashed a friendly smile. "Any sign of the Israelites?"

"Not yet," said the soldier.

"Perhaps the sight of such a big strong fellow has frightened them off." She gave a playful flick with the end of her kerchief. At the same moment she let it flutter down beside Moki.

"Boy," she called down, "bring me that scarf."

Moki took it and climbed the ladder. The sentry made a move, but she stepped quickly in front of him and whispered in Moki's ear, "Your friends say be hopeful. They will be here soon with the Israelites."

Moki slid down the ladder as if it were a firepole. Rahab stayed to flirt a while longer with the soldier and then returned to her house to signal Derek and Margo.

They had been sitting with their eyes fixed on the window. "Something must have gone wrong." Derek shifted his position.

"Look, a flash." Margo took a tiny piece of shiny metal from her pocket and returned the sign. "Now for her signal— There's one flash." After a long pause there was a second. "She's seen him . . . and . . ."

"He's OK," whooped Derek.

The welcome sound of the rams' horns at this moment added to their joy.

"The Israelites are coming at last!" they shouted together.

"The Israelites are coming at last," said the King of Jericho from his vantage place on the wall.

His captain stood beside him. "We shall hurl them back with ease, Sire."

The procession came into view. With the

guard and seven trumpeters in the lead, they moved to the road circling the city. Slowly they made their way around, the priests bearing the Ark of the Covenant and the armed men marching behind. There was no sound except the low-pitched notes of the horns.

On the wall the king watched and wondered. "What does this mean?" he whispered to the soldier beside him. Then, realizing how he was speaking, he shouted, "What are they doing? What is in that box?"

"I do not know, Sire. They carried it when the river stopped. If only the road were in reach of our bowmen, we would stop them." The captain shook his head.

The king stood up to get a better look. "It must be a magic box." Even as he watched, the column of Israelites completed their circuit and turned toward their camp.

"Look, they are retreating, Sire. Even with their box they cannot get through our great walls." But the captain's tone was uncertain.

"Why are they retreating before there is any action? I do not understand this. What are they up to?"

There was also uncertainty in the camp of Israel.

"A parade. That's all it was, a parade." Simeon slammed his fist into his palm. "Why?"

Joshua came up beside him. "You are troubled, Simeon. You may speak freely. You do not trust our plan."

Simeon turned to his leader, "We are wasting precious time. Every hour the people of Jericho are making their walls stronger. My men have trained with sword and spear; they have no use for parades. If we intend to take the city, we must use force. We must make war."

Joshua put a hand on Simeon's shoulder. "We are making war, my son. We are making war on their minds. We are sowing doubt."

Simeon shook his head with a smile. "War on their *minds*! I think I am rapidly losing my own!"

N ext day the same strange scene unfolded before the eyes of the king and his men who watched from atop the walls.

Margo and Derek slipped into the old shepherd's hut where they could watch the procession as it went round the city. Then just as before, the trumpeters and the bearers of the ark turned back toward the camp, followed by the silent company of soldiers.

"What are they doing?" roared the king.

"Marching." The captain was at the end of his patience. "They did the same thing yesterday."

"This is maddening." The king threw up his hands.

"Your Majesty, I have a suggestion. A spy has brought us a map of their encampment. We could attack them." The captain spread the parchment.

The king picked up his wine glass and drank deeply. "Perhaps that is what they want us to do. They are trying to trick us into coming out from behind our walls."

"But, Sire, because of our walls they may think we will not attack."

The king drank again from his stone cup. "Or, they may be thinking that we are thinking they —uh— they are thinking —uh— we won't . . . This is too much!" A sweep of his arm sent map and cup flying off the table and over to the wall.

Below Moki looked to see what made such a clatter, and what he saw gave him an idea. "Pen and ink and paper." When he was sure no one was looking, he spread the parchment on the ground, and dipping a piece of broken goblet into the wine, he wrote a message. Then he folded the parchment into a glider and waited for a chance to climb the wall and launch it.

Derek and Margo knew at once where the paper airplane came from. But as much as they wanted to know what he had to say, they waited until dark to pick it up. Then they ran back to camp.

"Let's see what he says." Margo unfolded the note: "Music is nice, but when is D-Day?"

"I'd like to know that myself." Derek took the paper. "Hey, look there's a map on the back."

They found Joshua just outside Simeon's tent. "Excuse me." Derek held out the map. "Our friend inside the city sent this. Is it important?"

Simeon was all attention. "It gives the layout of our camp. They must be planning to attack. Now we will have to fight."

"We will continue to follow the instructions of the Lord." Joshua nodded to Margo and Derek. "Good night."

And they did follow the instructions, the next day and the next and the next. Each day the citizens of Jericho grew more uneasy. The king and his soldiers were more and more bewildered.

"How long has this been going on?" asked the king. "They must have marched around with that cursed box at least a hundred times."

"Only six times, Sire. They must tire of this game soon."

Joshua addressed the Israelites that evening. "For six days we have taken the Ark of the Lord around the city of Jericho. We have followed our instructions carefully. Tomorrow we will take the city."

Simeon straightened his shoulders.

"My men stand ready to die for Israel."

"But you will not lose a single one," replied Joshua quietly. "Tomorrow we will circle the city seven times. At the seventh circuit, I will give a signal, and then all must shout for the glory of the Lord. The city will be ours."

Jebron bent down to Derek. "It will not be so good for your friend in the city. When we attack, they will surely kill him."

"Oh no, we can't let that happen. Come on, Margo." They ran off into the night.

Rahab appeared when she heard the stone against her shutter. "We have come to rescue Moki," whispered Margo. "Tomorrow the Israelites will take the city. You should make your plans to leave. Can you hide us?"

"The king's men are nervous and are watching everyone. But you might be safe under the flax of the roof. Come, I will help you conceal yourselves. In the morning you must go very early to get your friend. When you find him, run to the end of the main street and lift the wooden grating that covers the cave leading to our underground river. Go down the steps and follow the stream."

"Great." Derek shook her hand. "Thanks for everything."

Margo shook hands too. "Good luck to you, Rahab."

As soon as there was enough light, Margo and Derek made their way to the prison hut Rahab had showed them.

The door swung open and the overseer came out followed by a line of prisoners. Derek and Margo looked at each figure, but no Moki. Then, there he was at the end of the line. Moki gasped when Derek grabbed him, and the guards looked in their direction.

"Run!" Margo led the way down the main street.

"I know some back ways." Moki motioned them to follow him.

"Our friend on the wall sent you this bread." Derek handed him the loaf.

"Boy, am I hungry." Moki took a big bite and they ran on.

At the end of the street they found the grating and quickly ducked inside. There were narrow, moldy steps leading down into the black depths.

"Uh—oh," Moki darted back. "I dropped my bread."

"Forget it," warned Derek. But Moki was already at the top of the stairs. He lifted the grate and reached out. A dark shadow fell over him.

"Oh no, run for it," he shouted. "They've seen us."

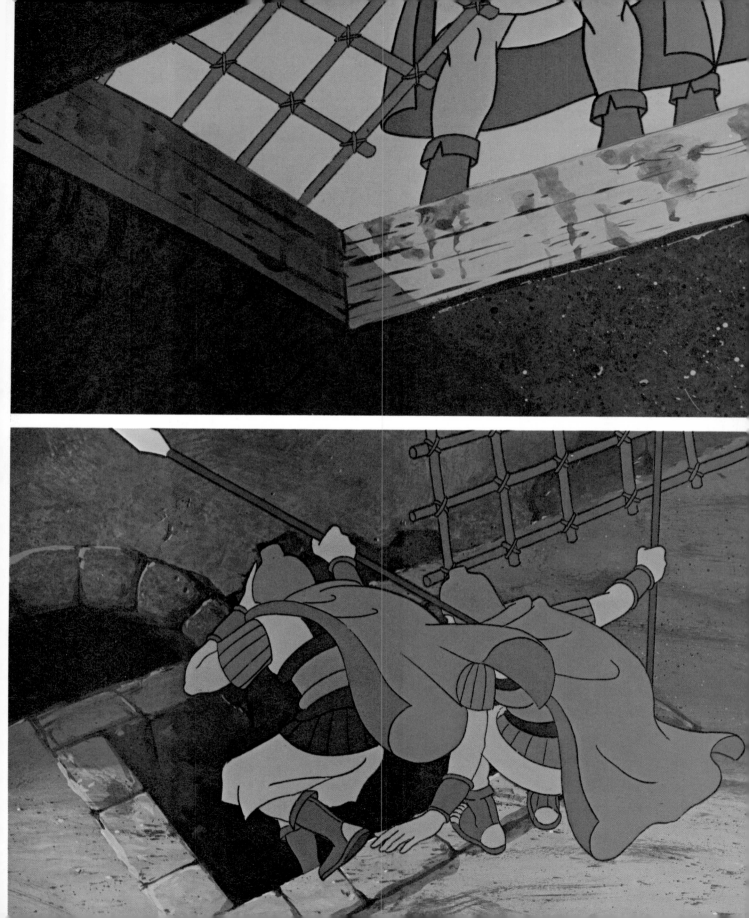

They went racing through the inky dark with the soldiers not far behind. The banks of the underground river were slippery, and in the blackness the three could feel that they were getting narrower and narrower, disappearing. Then, just as it seemed there was nowhere to go, in a pinpoint of light they saw a board across the water. They were over in a moment, and Derek stopped to pick up the plank.

"This will slow them down." He tucked it under his arm. "Besides we may need it."

Derek was right. Not a hundred yards farther on, the banks of the river vanished completely.

"Hop onto our surfboard," said Moki.

On the plain of Jericho, the familiar march around the city was taking place, but this day there was a difference. "What can this mean?" wondered the captain out loud. "Six times they have circled the city."

"They have never done this before," murmured the king, "and they are going around again."

Derek and Moki and Margo came bobbing out through the conduit in the side of the wall just in time to hear Joshua's voice, "Cry out now with all your might. Cry out for the glory of the Lord!"

Their voices roared and swelled into rolling waves of thunder.

The King of Jericho swayed as he put his
hands to his ears.

The bowmen lurched and fell as they
raised their arms to shoot.

Cracks began to appear in the walls
themselves, and great boulders broke away
and rumbled down. The booming was
everywhere, and the walls began to fall
apart.

The city crumbled in an avalanche of stone and rubble. A dense cloud hovered over the ruins, and there was a vast silence.